Praise for *The Secret to Selling Yourself Anytime, Anywhere: Start Bragging!*

This book was really valuable and not at all what I expected. It was so much more... Wow!

—CLT, job seeker

"Get Your Brag On" (webinar) was loads of fun and extremely thought-provoking. I thought I knew how to sell myself, AND this webinar opened my eyes to an even better way to do so. Thank you!!

—AVM, insurance employee

The best part of this book is that it is concise. Don't let the fact that this book is short fool you. I experienced a little resistance doing the exercises, but I persevered and I took my career up to a whole new level.

—ALS, SEO consultant

I did not think I needed this book. After all, I have been successfully networking and bragging about myself for over four decades. Yikes! When I learned that all her exercises were in the book, plus much, much more, I bought it. I loved the detailed instructions for making myself MUCH more appealing to my audience. I highly recommend this book, especially if you think you don't need it.

—LW, author and therapist

A book worth bragging about! I'd recommend it to those who need to improve their persuasion and influencing skills. The exercises are deceptively simple, but deliciously potent.

—International Review

THE SECRET TO SELLING YOURSELF ANYTIME, ANYWHERE

Start Bragging

JEANNETTE L. SEIBLY

**The Secret To Selling Yourself Anytime, Anywhere:
Start Bragging!**
by Jeannette L. Seibly

©2020 Jeannette L. Seibly

All Rights Reserved. No part of this book may be used or reproduced in any manner whatsoever without written permission, except in the case of brief quotations embodied in critical articles and reviews.

For information call Jeannette Seibly at 303-917-2993 or e-mail her at JLSeibly@SeibCo.com.

Published by
BizSavvy Books
PO Box 440112
Aurora, CO 80044

ISBN: 978-0-9847415-5-7 (Print)

Library of Congress Control Number: 2020911832

Editor: Faith Marcovecchio, Faith Marcovecchio Editorial
Book Coach: Judith Briles, The Book Shepherd
Book Design: Nick Zelinger, NZ Graphics

NOTE: Much of the material in this book appears under the title *It's Time to Brag! Career Edition.*

Third Edition
Printed in the United States of America

Also by Jeannette Seibly:

Hire Amazing Employees
It's Time to Brag! (First Edition)
Hire Amazing Employees, Second Edition
It's Time to Brag! Business Edition
It's Time to Brag! Career Edition

Author's Note

I've been touched, moved, and inspired by the successes and "wins" people have experienced by learning how to brag after completing the exercises in this book!

We all have many accomplishments.

Sadly, and too often, we're afraid to brag and share our achievements in a way that promotes us.

As a result, we lose out on winning the job offers, new assignments, promotions, and making more money!

It's not hard … you just have to complete the exercises outlined in this book and share your brags! I've also included worksheets in the back of this book to make it easy to complete the exercises. Or, you can go to *SeibCo.com/KTA/* to download the worksheet.

Now … *Get Your Brag On!*

Jeannette

Contents

Introduction 13

Chapter 1: Act Like a Cat 19

Chapter 2: The Key Ingredient 23

Chapter 3: Share Your Accomplishments 29

Chapter 4: Keep Writing! 35

Chapter 5: KTAs (Knowledge, Talents, Achievements) 39

Chapter 6: I AM 51

Chapter 7: Practice ... Practice ... Practice! ... 57

Chapter 8: Preparation for the All-Important Interview! 63

Chapter 9: Resumes Are for Marketing Purposes 69

Chapter 10: Networking Works! 73

Chapter 11: Career Transitioning 93

Chapter 12: Conduct Your Due Diligence 97

Chapter 13: Invaluable Career Wisdom! 101

About the Author 111

How to Work with the Author 113

KTAs (Worksheets can also be downloaded at
SeibCo.com/KTA/ 115

"No one wows a potential boss if they are unable to share their accomplishments in a business language that others readily understand."

— Jeannette L. Seibly

Introduction

You have only 4.3 minutes to be heard and positively noticed at the beginning of an interview.

It's up to you to create a remarkable and lasting impression.

Your ongoing success requires you talk with others in a biz-savvy manner!

A̲ll of us are taught at a very early age that bragging is wrong. It simply is not a nice thing to do. It's rude and shows poor manners. The fear is we will be thought of as braggarts!

We learned during our years growing up that we must be humble about our accomplishments ... often to our own detriment! We lose recognition when we don't step up to share our success. We get bypassed for promotions since others are unclear about our accomplishments. We are unable to clearly state our accomplishments in a job interview, and unaware of how to acquire "insider" information by networking with others.

> *A manager and her team were seated at a company function when her boss was called up front. The president of this multimillion-dollar marketing company acknowledged the boss for the work the manager and her team had accomplished. Imagine their surprise when the boss didn't mention them!*
>
> *Later, one on one and in private, the manager asked her boss, "Why didn't you acknowledge the team?"*
>
> *He responded, "Someday you will learn how to brag!"*

Our unwillingness to be in the spotlight stops us from achieving our career goals. This idea stays with us even as we are overlooked for promotions, key job assignments, or industry recognition.

What's missing? Not sharing our achievements in a biz-savvy manner.

Unfortunately, some falsely believe you simply need to "feel it" to develop a stronger self-image as a confident business professional. Confidence does not necessarily help you intuitively speak in a business-like manner, or speak up. Your confidence and competence naturally speak volumes when you are able to brag so others readily understand and value your results. They no longer dismiss your experiences and credentials, or fail to listen to how you can make a positive difference in the business environment.

There is a missing link!

When people interview for a job, they attempt to sound like others. If you are not able to distinguish yourself from everybody else with clarity, or if you sound too creative and people can't identify with your points, you've lost out on current and future opportunities.

We falsely believe we will obtain an insider view through networking interviews or informational interviews. That is a myth.

Networking is marketing, conducting research, educating yourself about different possibilities, and developing confidence and understanding of an industry, profession, or company.

Interviews are for selling yourself. You can't effectively do both at the same time. For that reason, you should not think of networking *meetings* as networking *interviews*.

We find it difficult to set up and conduct networking meetings because we have not differentiated ourselves in a way that makes others wish to talk with us. We forget people want to meet and know winners.

It's time to get over it! It's time to learn how to make a positive and lasting impression. In order for you to win the job or promotion or business recognition, you need to:

- Share your accomplishments in a biz-savvy manner

- Sell yourself in a successful interview to get the job offer

- Develop clarity to better understand a company's or industry's issues in networking meetings
- Be heard and be seen in a businesslike manner that compels others to take positive notice!

1
Act Like a Cat

"You can't sell yourself if you are unable to speak about your results in a businesslike manner."
—Jeannette Seibly

The key purpose of this book is to help you understand how to:

- Sell yourself in a job interview with ease and professionalism.

- Garner credibility faster in networking meetings and at other job-seeking events.

- Set up and manage effective networking meetings.

- Impress current and potential bosses with your value and accomplishments.

- Reap further interest in your employability when you answer the infamous interview question "Tell me about yourself".
- And most of all, be seen as confident and competent.

The picture below is to remind you how you look when you attempt to look like everyone else, sound like everyone else, or plagiarize others' accomplishments.

© Jeannette L. Seibly, 2013

Too often we pretend we are raccoons when in fact we're cats. Everyone knows we're cats. The raccoons know we're not one of them. The raccoons expect us to act like a cat when we are interacting with them. Obviously, as a cat you can never be a raccoon. Attempting to be someone you are not is unimpressive, even when you act in a respectful and tactful manner. Sadly, you hide your true abilities and accomplishments, and your uniqueness. As many times as I've shown this picture in my presentations, people actually miss seeing the difference between a cat and two raccoons! We don't necessarily hear the difference, either.

The point? People are less likely to hire you when they are unable to distinguish a difference between you and the many others competing for the position. Too often we keep talking because we misinterpret the interviewer's glazed-over look—if we even notice it at all—and instead see that look as interest in what we have to say.

Bosses hire people they feel comfortable with. Unfortunately, many don't handle the interview or selection process in a professional or equitable manner. It's up to you to make them comfortable while you share how you can help them be more successful. If you look and sound like everyone else, most hiring managers won't talk with you or do business with you in the future. If you're trying to be like everyone else, they will simply shut out everything you say and think, "I've heard it all before."

Whenever you hear yourself starting to sound like everyone else, stop it! Think of the cat and the raccoons. The picture is a friendly reminder that too often we like to hide out. It feels safer. However, hiding out won't pay the bills or earn you money or any well-deserved recognition. Nor will it win you a job or a promotion.

How do you show you're a winner? How do you wow them subtly but clearly while sharing your accomplishments?

Keep reading. Completing the exercises in *The Secret To Selling Yourself Anytime, Anywhere: Start Bragging!* will produce amazing results.

2
The Key Ingredient

On the next two pages, you will find two similar bios describing Jeannette Seibly, the author of this book. Read each one. Select the one you like best. Then ask yourself if you know the key difference between them.

INTRODUCTION #1:
About the Author

Jeannette Seibly is an internationally recognized award-winning executive coach and keynote speaker who has worked with entrepreneurs, executives, and business owners. She has helped lots of people work smarter, enjoy financial freedom, and realize their dreams NOW. She has an uncanny ability to help her clients identify roadblocks and focus on their goals to quickly produce unprecedented results. Each client has unique challenges, and Jeannette's gift is helping each one create success in his or her own unique way. She has guided the creation of millionaires and six-figure incomes.

Jeannette has a B.S. in personnel administration and M.A. in communications from Michigan State University.

She received the "People's Choice Award for Best Speaker" at the WE Local-Denver Society of Women Engineers event.

INTRODUCTION #2:
About the Author

Jeannette Seibly has been an internationally recognized business advisor and executive coach for over 27 years. She has helped thousands of entrepreneurs, executives, and business owners work smarter, enjoy financial freedom, and realize their dreams NOW.

Each client has unique challenges, and Jeannette's gift is helping each one create success in his or her own unique way. Along the way, she guided the creation of three millionaires and countless six-figure incomes.

During 2009, Jeannette conducted 13 Rewire Your Career workshops in three different venues. Many times the results were immediate, and used the same technology she is shares in *The Secret To Selling Yourself Anytime, Anywhere: Start Bragging!*

One person had an interview the next day and got the job offer two days later. Four women increased their sales, one by $20,000 in one and a half months. In recognition of her achievements, Jeannette received the "People's Choice Award for Best Speaker" at the WE Local-Denver Society of Women Engineers event.

As an author, she was written 7 books and published over 500 blog/article posts on current leadership and management challenges.

Jeannette has a B.S. in personnel administration and M.A. in communications from Michigan State University.

Which one did you like best?

Which sounded more professional? Did one convey credibility sooner than the other one? Which one pulled you into the conversation faster?

Most people will say #2.

What is the key difference? Many have a difficult time distinguishing it. They'll say, "Sounds more specific." "It's more interesting." "It's more descriptive." In fact, everything is similar except for one key ingredient!

The key ingredient?

The second one contained numbers, metrics, and results!

It bragged!

3
Share Your Accomplishments

If we sound like everyone else, nobody will listen.
They've already tuned us out!

But if we get too creative or different, nobody understands!
They won't take the time to find out!

The reality of why people are not interested?
They don't readily understand.

The challenge? To share the difference you provide.
Share your accomplishments!

When you present your results in a businesslike manner, it lets people know that you're a winner. People like to work with winners.

Relying upon rhetoric obtained from websites, self-help books, job seeker workshops, etc. will not differentiate you from others with the same or similar background, experience, and education. Showcasing your credentials is important to ensure people are interested in talking with you further. Remember, employers often believe their company is unique. If you get too creative as a way to distinguish yourself, nobody understands you. If they don't readily understand or you're unable to talk in basic business terms, they may question your business acumen and infer a lack of knowledge or integrity on your part.

The exercises in the upcoming chapters will address the following questions: What sets you apart? What do your past or current bosses respect you for? What is the positive and profound difference you've made for your coworkers, clients, and/or outside communities?

As stated earlier, trying to be a raccoon when you're a cat will not help you succeed!

The following is a paraphrased testimonial from a former client who is a serial entrepreneur. He started two businesses and failed because he was unable to differentiate effectively. Investors simply were not interested! After doing the exercises contained in this book, he sold his third and fourth businesses successfully. He's now working on number five.

> "I have always been impressed by people who are good at telling others what they accomplished in their career ... these people seemed amazing to me.
>
> When I wrote down and explained what I was good at ... looked at my own accomplishments ... I started to look pretty amazing myself." – HJ

As a job seeker or someone looking to be promoted, we can accomplish the same results when we learn how to brag!

Many times we're unconscious of what we do, how well we do it, and the difference it makes for our employers or others! We simply focus on getting the task done. We simply repeat the rhetoric we heard at a recent event. We simply tell people what we did in our past jobs—not as accomplishments, but simply as things we did because we were told or expected to do them.

When I introduce myself, if asked what I do I could say, "I am a coach." Too often that would be the end of any conversation. Everyone knows lots of coaches. Nothing new. Nothing inviting. Nothing distinguishing.

However, if I say, "I'm an executive coach who has created three millionaires" I have their attention! That statement invites them to continue the conversation. They ask questions and start a dialogue, *if* they are interested in learning more.

Some of you may think I'm talking about refining your elevator pitch. I'm not. It's more than that. Although you still need a one-liner, a.k.a. an objective for your resume, if you force it without doing the work contained in *The Secret To Selling Yourself Anytime, Anywhere: Start Bragging!*, that objective will sound stilted. When you've completed the assignments contained in *The Secret to Selling Yourself Anytime, Anywhere: Start Bragging!* you'll also have a supporting paragraph ready to share with others. It provides credibility and tells about your successes. It elicits interest and makes others want to learn more. It increases the possibility others will want to work with you!

It gets you hired!

It gets you referred to great opportunities!

It naturally builds your confidence.

This process creates a huge breakthrough. It allows you to truly see what you've accomplished. It is the first step in learning how to brag in a businesslike manner.

Remember, luck is in your preparation! Are you prepared?

Let's get started!

4
Keep Writing!

**The key is to keep writing.
Don't stop after writing down
a couple of things.
Keep writing!
When you think you're done,
keep writing!
When you can't think of the answers,
keep writing.
Trust the process—the breakthroughs
will come.**

In this chapter and the next, there are five steps and exercises to move your thinking toward what you have accomplished. Don't make it harder than it is.

Simply keep writing, even when you think you're finished.

Initially, you may believe the exercises are too simple. Don't be fooled by their simplicity! Many people have, and consequently neglected to do their work. Some were confronted by writing down their responses. Others by focusing on their achievements. Although these sound like simple things to do, it's hard when it's about you. I've had people simply toss the exercises aside, never to work on them again. I've had people cry! I've had people stop, then pick up the pen again and write some more. Eventually, they had their breakthrough.

It's all in the writing. It's getting your brain to realize that you've accomplished more by writing it all down. This process takes your accomplishments out of your unconscious and forces you to think through your results. And each of you has had many! The process makes people become conscious of them.

When I was conducting a webinar for job seekers, a young man, age 17, was there. When it came

> *time to write, he was stumped. He didn't believe he had achieved anything, being so young. I shared with him that everyone, regardless of their age or background or work experience, has accomplished something. I made a couple of suggestions to get him started. About 10 minutes later, he asked for more worksheets! It was amazing to see his beaming smile. He learned to brag!*

It's all in doing the work! Do not get ahead of the instructions. Write down everything you think of. Ignore your mental monologue about its worthiness. No one else will see this work; unless, of course, you show them!

All of us have a multitude of unconscious reasons why we can't brag. It's an attitude we've developed over our entire lives, and that attitude is why it's difficult for us to share our great results. Writing them down is the first step. These five simple exercises will help provide a structure to get you writing! When you are conscious of your successes, there is a natural difference in how you communicate with others. Again, it cannot be forced. Shortcuts rarely have any lasting effects.

5

KTAs
(Knowledge, Talents, Achievements)

Step One:
Knowledge: What do you know?

The following are ideas to get you started. They are not inclusive. The breakthrough will only be as good as the writing you do. If you are unable to write, have someone else scribe for you. Or use transcription software that writes down what you are saying. Regardless of your age or life experiences, you've accomplished many things in your life. Simply write them all down!

NOTE: Worksheets are provided in back of this book. Or, you can download the Worksheets at *SeibCo.com/KTA/*

Knowledge	Talents	Achievements
Software		
Engineering		
Human Resources		
Parenting		
Grandparenting		
Accounting		
Financial Reporting		
Perennial Gardening		
Cake Decorating		

* The above are simply examples to get you started.

Step Two: Talent: Use a verb to describe your knowledge.

You can write down more than one talent to describe your knowledge. Keep them simple. The following are ideas to get you started. They are not inclusive. The breakthrough will only be as good as the writing you do. Regardless of your age or life experiences, you've accomplished many things in your life. Simply write them down!

Knowledge	Talents	Achievements
Software	**Code mobile apps**	
Engineering	**Conduct propery surveys**	
Human Resources	**Conduct interviews** **Manage employee benefits** **Communicate compensation changes**	

NOTE: Worksheets are provided in back of this book. Or, you can download the Worksheets at *SeibCo.com/KTA/*

Knowledge	Talents	Achievements
Parenting	**Coach Little League**	
Fundraising	**Sell chocolate bars for 4-H** **Wash cars for Boy Scouts**	

NOTE: Worksheets are provided in back of this book. Or, you can download the Worksheets at *SeibCo.com/KTA/*

* The above are simply examples to get you started.

Step Three:
Achievements: Use two numbers to show your results.

Achievements are where the rubber meets the road. We use two numbers to show the results we have achieved that made a positive difference. Simply talking about a task isn't inspiring to others. Achievements are why people hire you, why companies consider you a top performer. Too often people's resume will say, "Answered phones. Processed claims. Troubleshoot software development issues." These don't tell us anything unique. They're examples of simply being a cat attempting to look like a raccoon!

We have conditioned our brains not to think in terms of numeric results. Numeric results require getting into the details of what you've accomplished. Doing this level of work allows you to be more proficient when communicating your accomplishments, even though you will not be communicating all the details! When people communicate unconsciously, they are often glib, gloss over important points, and speak in a manner others don't understand. After completing these exercises, you will naturally be communicating at a more conscious level, sharing work and life experiences in a way others can relate to. That will help you get hired or promoted or given great work assignments!

You can write down more than one achievement to describe each talent. The following are ideas to get you started. They are not inclusive. The breakthrough will only be as good as the writing you do. Regardless of your age or life experiences, you've accomplished many things in your life. Simply write them down!

The following are examples to get you started.

Knowledge	Talents	Achievements
Software	**Code mobile apps**	**Created a customer service app for a $2MM company in three business days. Troubleshot with five clients when $150,000 software package**

Knowledge	Talents	Achievements
Software (cont.)		failed to produce the results promised. Worked with three testers and developers to find the problem and resolved it within three days.
Engineering	Conduct property surveys	Conducted 10 surveys for state highway department and saved $2M on one project.
Human Resources	Conduct interviews	Conducted 20 interviews of Systems Engineers in two days. Reduced turnover from 125% to 25% in one year.

NOTE: Worksheets are provided in back of this book. Or, you can download the Worksheets at *SeibCo.com/KTA/*

Knowledge	Talents	Achievements
Human Resources (cont.)	Manage employee benefits	Handled the implementation of two benefit programs for 360 employees. Terminated one pension plan to recoup over-funding of $1.3M without any loss of benefits to the retirees.
	Communicate compensation changes	Worked with a unionized group of 40 employees to communicate the new hourly wage, $20/hour to $19.50/hour. This was completed without a strike and provided employees the

Knowledge	Talents	Achievements
Human Resources (cont.)		opportunity to see with monthly bonuses they could earn $22/hour.
Parenting	Coach Little League	Coached fifteen 12-year-olds to win the city league by competing against five different teams.
Fundraising	Sell chocolate bars	Top seller of 100 candy bars for 4-H, providing the 4-H Chapter $500 dollars to spend on a trip to Washington DC.
	Wash cars for Boy Scouts	Participated in car wash to raise $5,000 to benefit 30 underprivileged children.

* The above are simply examples to get you started.

Keep writing! Many of you will not readily know your numbers. That's not a problem. Simply write down your thoughts. After you are done writing, conduct research with former coworkers or bosses, current clients, friends, and family. Although most people will not investigate your numbers, you want to be as truthful as possible. If you are caught in a lie, it could easily hurt your ability to attract new job opportunities or win recognition from your employer or an outside organization.

As one participant said after struggling with numbers, "We all have numbers to describe our successes. It's simply becoming present to the difference we made and the results we accomplished."

The key? Stay out of mental monologues telling you this is too hard, you don't like working with numbers, or you don't believe you should have to do the work. Writing this information down will show you what you've accomplished thus far in your life. You've got years of false conditioning telling you it's not OK to brag or it's poor business manners to share your successes and achievements. Now is the time to blast through those walls, which have hindered your career, business recognition, and credibility.

The fact that you are aware of your numbers (a.k.a. results) and are able to communicate them appropriately will definitely provide you with the advantage. Doing so will set you apart from the pack. It's like being the cat among the raccoons instead of pretending to be a raccoon.

Let me offer you some tips on how to think about your numbers. Remember, numbers can be expressed in percentages, actuals, and approximations (i.e., realistic guesstimates). Not everything is quantifiable; for example, it is difficult to measure happiness in the employees you managed, even though that may interest some employers. But what you can measure is impressive: Most prospective employers will be far more interested in how many projects you achieved on time and within budget. What was the budget? How long did it take to complete the project while working with and through others? What setbacks arose? How did you handle them? Did you have any turnover? Those are things that can be measured.

You may be confronted with this part of the exercise. Keep writing! I had one woman cry through the whole exercise, but she persisted. Within two weeks, she was re-employed after being unemployed for almost 18 months.

6
I AM ...

"Effectively communicate who you are and the value you can provide."
—Jeannette Seibly

Step Four:
I AM ...

Don't work on this until after you've completed at least several pages of the KTAs (Knowledge, Talents, and Achievements).

In twenty words or less, describe who you are. Keep it simple and smart.

Start with the phrase, **"I am ... "**

Don't be too creative. People won't understand you or be able to readily connect with you. As a rule of thumb, ask yourself if a 12-year-old could easily understand what you just said. If you MUST explain in order to be understood, it's not simple enough. Furthermore, if you have to explain, many people will assume you are being defensive—another reason people stop listening!

For example, I could say, "I am a coach who helps others get out of their own way." There are no numbers. And that may not be enough to generate interest in how I can help someone. However, if I say, "I am an executive coach who has guided the creation of three millionaires" or "I'm a hiring expert who has helped one company reduce turnover from 125 percent to 25 percent," now I've got the hiring manager's attention.

Stay away from clichés such as "I help people feel great!" or "I help companies become successful."

Don't hide the fact of what you do. If you're an administrative assistant seeking a promotion, you might say, "I am a professional assistant and help my bosses get their jobs done with ease."

If you are a waiter and want a customer service job, you could say, "I am a customer service professional who achieves 100 percent customer satisfaction."

It helps people to readily identify with your unique qualities. This specific information, based upon what you have been successful in accomplishing with your past bosses, will be of interest to your prospective boss.

Unless someone asks you a question, providing additional information after you've made your initial statement is like talking to the wall! They will not be listening! Wait until a question is asked and answer it directly with additional results.

Plan to fine-tune this all-important "I am ..." statement. You may need to test it out on several people. Work with a job coach or a marketing or PR friend to help you.

Some of you will be frustrated; this information doesn't necessarily come out the first time you write it down. Or the second time. Or the third. Keep in mind that in most cases our brains have been trained to hide out and play small. Or, if we come from a different place, we've trained our brains to spin the facts or be highly creative. Although this may help satisfy our egos, it won't help us attract positive attention! Prospective employers must be able to readily and easily identify with how we can help them. Make sure you're using simple business words like "business advisor" or "executive coach" or "software engineer" or "virtual assistant" or "business owner" or "CPA." It helps others to easily understand us much faster. Stay away from cute or faddish jargon.

Straight talk can produce job or promotion opportunities. Imagine how frustrated you would be if someone started a conversation with something like, "I'm looking for a sales job," and only after further conversation did you learn that the man wasn't interested in closing any sales deals, he was simply looking for estimating or pricing jobs. Talk straight!

Step Five:
My background includes … "

This is where you bring it all together. Write one to two paragraphs to describe your **"I am …"** statement. Customize it for the audience. USE the NUMBERS!!!

Keep it short and to the point. Most people, including interviewers, have short attention spans. If you're unable to grab their attention, you will probably not receive the job offer or promotion you wanted.

For example, one paragraph at a networking meeting will work. The purpose of a networking meeting isn't to interview for a job. It's simply to create the interest to talk further.

Writing a well-worded paragraph or two will tell others about your success!

Customize it for your audience and use those numbers. It's amazing to me that we spend time clarifying numbers and then they are not used. You may wish to review my two bios in Chapter 2. In the first I didn't use numbers, but in the second I did. See the difference?

In an interview, tailor your paragraphs to the position being offered. Keep it to one or two minutes. I remember one time when a person talked for 15 minutes during an interview when asked the infamous question "Tell us about yourself." We were all so bored with him that the outcome of his interview was readily determined at that point: NO!

You may wish to hire a job coach, PR person, or

marketing person to help you write or edit. Do not allow them to replace the numbers. They may have not learned how to brag yet! It's commonplace that people feel uncomfortable using numbers.

Or, you could have a raving fan of your talents (for example a coworker, client, or boss) write it up for you, and then you could edit it.

The point? Take the time to write and fine-tune. Remember, your statement will need to be modified for the company, industry, or profession you are applying to. Take time to network with others. Find out what key qualities the business you're interested in requires that are not listed in their job postings. For example, speaking to a group of job seekers about interviewing is not the same as speaking to a group of business owners needing to hire employees. Tailor your introduction accordingly. Don't forget: It's critical to build credibility in order for them to listen to your message. It makes all the difference!

7

Practice … Practice … Practice!

Like anything, mastery takes practice. Don't beat yourself up if you stumble or take the easy road by not using your numbers. Simply review and practice in front of the mirror. Keep doing your "mirror work" until the person looking back at you in the mirror gets it. If this was easy to do, I wouldn't have spent time writing a book about it.

> *I met a young professional wishing to be a realtor. She had the education and licenses. However, when she talked with people, she looked at her feet! She purchased* The Secret to Selling Yourself Anytime, Anywhere: Start Bragging! *and completed the five exercises. The next time I saw her, she made eye contact, shook my hand*

> *confidently, and clearly articulated her successes in helping others find their dream homes. She had learned how to brag and her new confidence radiated!*

You may get frustrated. You may be confronted. You may wish to be the cat trying to look like the raccoons. However, eventually you'll get hungry enough to want the breakthrough.

If it's too confronting, take small steps. Write down only one KTA each day. Share it with only one person per day.

You may have insights about accomplishments while you are driving to an appointment or lying in bed at night. Write them down! This flood of additional information may help you in the next network meeting or on the next job interview or conversation with your boss. (No, they don't know all the results you've achieved for the company!)

The goal is to have people better understand who you are and identify with what you can provide for them. This understanding builds credibility faster. It will set the tone for your success!

During the course of an interview or any type of presentation, you should plan to use your KTAs to help you answer the interviewer's questions. A little bit of repetition can help if you need to restate a particular point, such as using a different set of numbers or examples.

When writing a resume, since most interviewers only skim them because of the hundreds of resumes they receive, be sure your first paragraph summarizes your achievements. Use your numbers! You want to entice them to read further.

I've read thousands of resumes in my decades of experience in hiring people and coaching clients during their selection processes. Most are poorly written and don't convey what the company needs. I suggested to one applicant that he include numbers and results after he asked me how to improve his resume. His response? He needed to keep it to two pages! Rewriting a

> *resume with results will not increase the length of your resume unless you are being long-winded. Remember: Resumes are written to market to prospective employers. Think from their point of view.*

This process works! When you share your brag statements, be responsible for your tone of voice, ego, and attitude. Coming across as a braggart, regardless of whether you're a professional woman or man, will not help you. Coming across apologetically or mumbling will not work either. Simply share your successes in a straightforward manner. Ensure your attitude is positive and helpful. Keep it simple! Humility goes a long way.

Stay away from sharing any details of how you achieved the numbers until you get to that point in your interview.

The goal is for prospective employers to appreciate your expertise and to hear how you helped past employers or clients fix an issue or pursue an opportunity. You want them to understand how you can do the same for them based upon their needs. This level of conversation is normally required before being offered a job. People want to work with winners! Winners know how to share their achievements in a professional manner that works.

Your ability to communicate your successes using numbers will forever alter the way you think and speak. You should see results quickly. Have fun sharing. Enjoy bragging! You've earned it!

8

Preparation for the All-Important Interview!

The reality is that many companies do a very poor job of interviewing job candidates. Many interviewers are unprepared or simply unclear regarding what questions to ask to determine a candidate's skills and job fit.

That doesn't mean you shouldn't be prepared!

Prior to any interview, connect with your network to find out the real issues of the company are. A job posting simply lets you know the basic requirements. There is unwritten information you need to ascertain and be prepared to discuss in a biz-savvy manner. Simply saying, "I can do it" will not cause them to offer you the job. You need to share your brag statements.

On the next page is an interview outline (taken from *Hire Amazing Employees, Second Edition*). Every company has its own set of questions. This is simply one set of questions to use in preparation for each and every interview. Never wing it! If you've practiced, you should be able to handle the variety of questions you are asked.

When you prepare, write out your answers! Remember, this is critical. Include your work and numbers from the brag exercises. I'm always amazed by people spending time on these critical exercises and then failing to include their numbers, metrics, and results in their preparation. If you are prepared, there's a greater chance you will wow them in the interview. It is how job offers and promotions are created.

Practice in front of the mirror (yes, look into the mirror when you are answering the questions—eye contact is very important). Also, have one or two close friends or family members ask you the questions and critique your responses.

Interview Outline

Pre-Screen Interview (usually conducted via phone or video conferencing)

1. Tell me your exact dates of employment for each position.

2. Breakdown your base salary, overtime, bonus, and other compensation.

3. Why did you leave each of your former employers?

4. Tell me about yourself and your professional background.

5. What is your current salary? (or recent salary, if unemployed)

6. What are your salary expectations?

7. What are you looking for in your next position?

8. Why are you leaving your present position? (if currently employed)

9. Why did you leave your former employer? (if currently unemployed)

10. What type of work environment are you looking for?

11. Please describe any work experience with _____ industry.

In-Person Interview (usually conducted on site or via video conferencing)

1. Tell me about your work experience in _____. *(Prepare four to seven answers in different areas of importance based on the job posting and networking feedback.)*

2. Name three of your strengths and why you believe they are strengths.

3. Name three weaknesses or areas where you could improve. *(Everyone has them! Saying you don't makes you sound unaware of yourself or arrogant.)*

4. Why are these important?
5. How do you handle mistakes?
6. How would you describe your work habits?
7. Describe your leadership experience and how you feel that experience will benefit you in this job.

8. If I were to talk with others, how would they describe you?
    a. Coworkers?
    b. Subordinates?
    c. Bosses?
    d. Customers?
9. Is there anything else you can tell me that you believe is important that we haven't covered?

10. Do you have any questions? *(It's time for you to "Conduct Your Due Diligence," see Chapter 12. Always be sure to have questions to ask for each and every interviewer! They should be the same questions for each interviewer within a company to see if you are getting the same or similar responses. Beware of dissimilar information and* ask *questions to clarify.)*

9

Resumes Are for Marketing Purposes

On average, recruiters only spend six seconds skimming your resume. Many companies today want you to have all the skills posted, plus other qualities not listed. With everything seemingly stacked against you, how do you win the interview?

Include your results (a.k.a. numbers or metrics) in the resume. Keep it to two pages. Make sure to stay away from words like "integrity," "high-level," "trustworthy," etc. These words are meaningless. Use your numbers, metrics, and results to create the impression that you are someone they need to talk to! After you write your initial draft, have a marketing person review it and offer comments. Remember, resumes will only market you. You must sell yourself in person, phone interviews, and via other contact.

Pick the best resume outline that showcases you!

- A functional resume is focused on your achievements, education, and skills.
- A chronological resume lists your jobs in the order that you held them.

Many employers like the chronological resume better to see your most up-to-date skills.

Be sure to use your number, metrics, and other results. *Using the brag statements will encourage employers to stop skimming and start reading!*

> A great idea! Create a historical document listing all your work history, job responsibilities, and education.
>
> Then, for each job you are applying for, only list those skills, job responsibilities, and education the company is seeking.
>
> Since companies rely on "automated keyword searches" before actually reading the resume, use and spell the words exactly as they appear in the job posting for your cover letter and resume.

Functional Resume

NAME

Address   Phone:
Cell:
Email:

SUMMARY

PROFESSIONAL EXPERIENCE

Pick three primary areas of focus

EMPLOYMENT HISTORY

Title of Position, Company Name, City, State, Dates of Employment

AWARDS AND SELECTED PROFESSIONAL AFFILIATIONS

EDUCATION

Chronological Resume

NAME

Address   Phone:
                                                       Cell:
                                                       Email:

SUMMARY

PROFESSIONAL EXPERIENCE

List most recent employer first, going back at least 10 years.
Include Title of Position, Company Name,
City, State,
Dates of Employment

AWARDS AND SELECTED PROFESSIONAL AFFILIATIONS

EDUCATION

10

Networking Works!

What is networking?

Networking is simply talking with others to:

- Investigate new possibilities
    - Become aware of new types of jobs and skills required
    - Explore new opportunities such as:
        - new technologies
        - new companies
        - new products
        - new occupations
        - new human relation/diversity concerns
        - environmental changes
        - ethical considerations and new business practices required due to global competition

Most people will have more than seven careers in their lifetimes—not just one—so stay current! Don't forget that new possibilities are being created daily.

- Educate yourself about new opportunities
  - Tap into 90 percent of the world's information, which is in people's heads!
- Explore opportunities and conduct due diligence
  - Contact others for information regarding best practices and policies, critical issues, possible solutions, etc.
  - Create new opportunities for yourself by staying current on issues and possible solutions
- Evaluate options and prepare to negotiate
  - Make better decisions about the job, company, industry, compensation package, etc.
  - Make transitioning easier into a different type of work or industry

What are the added benefits of networking?

- Develops lifelong contacts so you can have a great career now and in the future
- Keeps you up-to-date on industry and professional changes
- Allows you to achieve your personal and professional goals faster
- Helps you resolve issues quicker and more effectively
- Taps you into unpublished jobs and creates new opportunities.

Why do we make networking difficult?
We are unclear about the difference between networking and interviewing.
There is no such thing as a networking interview:
You cannot network and interview at the same time.

It's similar to the difference between marketing and sales.

- Marketing is:
  - Researching issues and solutions
  - Collecting information necessary to sell
  - Finding new opportunities
  - Educating yourself and others
  - Sending out a resume
- Sales is:
  - Presentation (e.g., the interview)
  - Determining job fit (e.g., due diligence)
  - Closing the deal (e.g., getting the job offer and negotiating salary, benefits, perks, and/or work requirements)

The clear distinction:

- Networking is marketing.
- Interviewing is selling.

Fine-tune your clarity:

- You cannot sell and market at the same time.
- You can't sell if you don't understand the employer's needs (i.e., do your market research).

- Companies hire you for their own reasons, not yours.

You may ask, "Is an informational interview or networking interview helpful?" The short answer is no.

Why?

To win a job interview, we need to know the unpublished information. The purpose of networking is to tap into the 90 percent of information that is not published. The term "networking interview" implies that the potential employer will ask all the questions. Potential employers do not normally share a lot of insider information. In any interview, there is an implied understanding that the interviewer will be asking the questions. They will be ascertaining whether or not they like you, think you might fit in their company, or think you would be a good fit working with a friend or business associate in another company. In less than 4.3 minutes, they will have unconsciously made a yes or no determination about whether they would hire you. If their determination is a no, that limits your ability to find out more about the company, industry, or profession. And it severely limits your ability to receive introductions into their network!

How to Do It

To keep your power and confidence, it's important that you understand and come prepared to run a networking meeting! Doing so increases your opportunity to trade information and learn about the person you are meeting with, his or her company, the profession, or the industry. Understanding and preparation on your part also prevent the person you're talking to from making a snap judgment on whether or not they would hire you.

> *Important Note: Do not email or provide a resume before, during or after a networking meeting. Why? When you schedule your meeting, you need to indicate that you do not expect this to be a job interview. When you produce a resume, you give the impression that you lied! That will limit future opportunities with the person you're talking to and with his or her company.*

Keys to Conduct Effective Networking Meetings:

- You are establishing contacts who are valuable sources of information.
- You are seeking information regarding issues and potential solutions.
- You are not asking for a job.
- You are not expecting the person you're speaking with to know of one.

How Do I Get Started?

Make it easy. Start with references:

- ✓ former bosses
- ✓ previous coworkers
- ✓ family
- ✓ professional and personal acquaintances
- ✓ social network contacts

Remember, geography is not important.

Check out social media sites and websites to supplement conversations with others.

How to Initiate a Meeting:

- Send an introduction email. Or, better yet, pick up the phone and call. You can also send a letter requesting a meeting.
- If you are using email, keep it short—a couple of paragraphs. In the "Subject" line, indicate "Referred by … "
- If you're making a phone call, use a written script that you have practiced.
- If you're writing a letter, keep it to one page. Be sure to proofread it!
- NEVER include a resume.
- Never just stop by a company to set up a meeting, even if you already know the person!
- Meetings should be no longer than 20 minutes.

How to Schedule the Meeting:

Here is language you can use to open your email, letter, or script for a phone call. Keep in mind that if you send an email or letter, it is your responsibility to follow up with a call to schedule the meeting. If you contact the person via phone, it's up to you to request the meeting.

- ✓ I am …. *(use the "I am … " statement you have developed. Do not include any words such as "job seeker.")*
- ✓ When speaking with X *(include the name of the person who referred you)*, we discussed …
- ✓ He or she mentioned you would be a valuable source of information on this topic.
- ✓ I would welcome the opportunity to meet with you.
- ✓ My background includes … *(2 to 3 sentences – be sure they are on point with the topic to be discussed).*
- ✓ I do not expect you to know of a job; this is simply an opportunity for me to learn more about …

- ✓ I will contact you on X to set up a convenient time to talk. *(Be sure you follow up!)*

The Actual Meeting: First Impressions Matter!

- ✓ Arrive 5–10 minutes early.
- ✓ Dress professionally. Be clean and neat.
- ✓ Don't chew gum.
- ✓ To help connect with the person faster, wear a tie/scarf, suit, or shirt/blouse that matches your eye color.
- ✓ Always be nice to the receptionist, assistant, or the server at the restaurant or coffee shop.
- ✓ Shake hands and provide a business card.
- ✓ Leave your resume at home!
- ✓ If using video conferencing, ensure your system is working before meeting. Remove any wall art that may be considered offensive. Limit noise from kids, pets, or loud neighbors.

The Actual Meeting: Getting Off on the Right Foot

- ✓ Introduce yourself by clearly stating your first and last names.
- ✓ Extend your hand for a handshake.
- ✓ Make a statement about the person who introduced you by stating that person's full name and add that he or she said, "you would be a valuable source of information."

The Actual Meeting: The Meeting!

This is where most people lose control of the networking meeting and the other person turns it into a yes or no interview.

- ✓ Thank them for meeting with you.
- ✓ Restate the full name of the person who referred you and add that "they said you would be a valuable source of information." (Yes, this is an intentional repeat.)

- ✓ Reiterate the time frame for the meeting: "As I shared when setting up this meeting, I plan on taking about 20 minutes and have specific questions to ask."
- ✓ Remind them you are not here for an interview: "I am seeking new career opportunities and do not expect you to know of any job openings at this time."
- ✓ State the intention of the meeting: "I am seeking company and industry information that can support me in exploring new opportunities."
- ✓ Set the tone. Share your "I am …" and "My background includes … " statements.

Ask questions designed to answer the following. Use a conversational tone; this is not an interrogation!

- ✓ What is the person's background, years in their profession, years in the industry, etc.?
- ✓ What are three problems or needs of the industry, profession, or company?

✓ What are three possible solutions, qualifications required to address them, company's interest in resolutions?

The Actual Meeting: Summary

✓ Recap the top three issues discussed and your background in those areas.

✓ Request specific suggestions for furthering your employment campaign:

- ➤ "How do you feel my background would fit into this company, industry, or profession?"

- ➤ "What are your suggestions for ways to conduct my job search campaign?"

- ➤ "What are your ideas for utilizing my background?"

The Actual Meeting: Asking for Referrals

Ask who they would recommend that you speak with next:

- "Of the people you are professionally or personally associated with, who would you recommend I talk with further about _____?"
- "Could you suggest other people you are professionally associated with to talk to about _____?"

Note: Be aware of being referred to recruiters. If you find this happening often, you may be talking with people who cannot help you or don't feel comfortable with you, or you have failed to properly network with them.

The Actual Meeting: End of Meeting

- Thank them for their time.
- If it's a face-to-face meeting, shake hands and leave. Do NOT leave a resume. DO leave a business card.
- If it's a conference video meeting, end the meeting with a smile. Do NOT send a resume. DO send a thank you email.

After the Meeting

- Send the person a written thank you email, letter, or card within 24 hours.
- Include any information that you promised to provide.
- Send a thank you to the person who referred you. They may have additional contacts for you to talk with.

Review – Part I (Immediately Afterwards)

- ✓ Who did I talk with: title, background, company?
- ✓ What did I learn about the department, company, industry, profession, issues, company or industry jargon?
- ✓ Where are the problems and issues for the company, department, industry, or profession?
- ✓ What are possible solutions?

✓ How does this fit my experience, education, goals, and interests?

Review – Part II (After 24 Hours)

✓ What changes do I need to consider for my goals (either immediate or future)?

✓ Am I asking the right questions?

✓ Am I getting the type of information I need?

✓ If not, who do I talk with?

✓ Do I need to update my "I am … " and "My background includes …" statements?

Do

✓ Be prepared with an agenda.

✓ Treat this as an important meeting.

✓ Ask and expect referrals.

✓ Actively listen.

✓ Be coachable.

- ✓ Practice, practice, practice before each meeting.
- ✓ Determine a weekly goal of meetings if you are unemployed, and follow-through.
- ✓ Update your social media sites (e.g., LinkedIn, Facebook, Twitter, etc.) weekly with positive comments.

Don't

- ✓ Fall into the interview trap.
- ✓ Provide a resume.
- ✓ Get defensive.
- ✓ Get into political or religious discussions.
- ✓ Vent your frustrations.
- ✓ Post inappropriate comments on your social media sites.
- ✓ Conduct meetings with high-level decision-makers without having conducted at least three other networking meetings previously.

Keep your network alive and well. Networking works when you stay in touch with others and are available if they need anything. If you only contact your network when you need something, others will stop helping you!

Effective networking means you can work smarter, not harder. Too often people who effectively conduct networking meetings enjoy it! Beware of the trap of confusing lots of activity with achieving your intended result: finding your next employer.

Questions to ask yourself:

- ✓ Are you getting the types of introductions that fit your goals?
- ✓ Are you getting closer to finding current job openings or new opportunities that are not posted? If not, what do you need to transform?
- ✓ Talk with your coach, mentor, or friend for insight. We all have blind spots. It takes someone else's insight to help us see more clearly.

11

Career Transitioning

Changing from one job to a different type of work, industry, or profession requires taking an inventory of your brag statements.

There is a prerequisite for the following exercise: You will need to know the key job duties and responsibilities in the positions you are interested in pursuing. Also, you will need to have completed your brag statements to make this next exercise meaningful.

Most companies love to think they are unique. It's simply their way of weeding out prospective applicants. Unfortunately, they miss a lot of great candidates that way. It's up to you to understand their requirements by reading the company's job postings, website, press releases (usually found on the Internet), and talking with your network. Then use what you have learned in a biz-savvy manner in networking meetings, on resumes, and when other opportunities arise.

Based upon the information you've gleaned, make a list of the written and unwritten requirements of the job you're applying for. Then add your brag statements. Be sure they are specific and on point. Some examples:

List of Requirements	**Your Corresponding Brag Statements**
Industry GAAP	Have 20 years of accounting experience in five different industries.
Recruiting	Have 10 years of recruiting experience and have hired 10 software engineers for a $10MM technology company.

List of Requirements	**Your Corresponding Brag Statements**
Call Center	Have worked at a major retailer's customer help desk for two years, handling 1,000s of returns over the phone with no complaints.

Then, prepare for the interview or networking meetings using this newly configured data.

12

Conduct Your Due Diligence

Too often in our haste to get a job, promotion, or new opportunity, we fail to stop and consider what we need. If we don't ask, we won't receive. Blaming your new boss or employer for not magically knowing or mind-reading what you need will only create dissatisfaction. Take time to conduct your own due diligence.

Before the Interview

Read the company website. Google the name of the company and its products and services. Google the name of the interviewer(s). Contact your network for information that is not published (remember, 90 percent of the world's information is in other people's heads!). Check out both the company and interviewer(s) their social media information (e.g., LinkedIn, Facebook, Twitter, etc.). Subscribe to their feeds to see what you can learn about their products and services.

During the Interview

Most interviewees make huge mistakes by assuming they know how a company operates. Since you've never worked for this company, boss, or team members, have good business questions ready to ask. Ask them!

Write them down and take the list with you. Some ideas to get you started:

- What results will the successful incumbent achieve in the first 30 days? 60 days? 90 days? 180 days? (If they are unrealistic, it will negatively impact your longevity and satisfaction with the job.)

- What resources are available?

- What new opportunities need to be created?

- Who will the successful incumbent report to? Who will report to him or her?

- What type of clients does the company have (be sure you've done your investigation) and what type of challenges or issues might the company be experiencing?
- What are the top three challenges of the job?
- What do they believe are the solutions?

Keep in mind that some employers will lie to keep you interested, or because they fear you will tell others. Confidentiality is important on your part.

When the Position Is Offered

Prior to being offered this position, determine what your top three must-haves are. Write them down. Plan on making these requests when you are offered the position, not after you're employed. Remember, once you've requested them, you cannot add additional wants. Don't forget to ask for clarity (and in writing) about salary, benefits, and the specifics of those benefits. What is the length of time before benefits begin? How is vacation or other personal time calculated?

Retirement? Other benefits? Will those benefits include family members?

13

Invaluable Career Wisdom!

It's an Attitude: Your Attitude Is an Asset or a Liability. It's Your Choice.

During this process, your attitude will define how others see you and if they will provide you with the type of contacts that make a difference for you. A positive attitude influences your career options, now and in the future. This is why some people get opportunities even though they have lesser qualifications than you.

Brag statements, network, interview and negotiating skills are important if you want to have a satisfying career and develop yourself over your lifetime. They are great reflections of a positive and confident attitude, when you share them. Gone are the 30-year-and-out jobs that many of our parents and grandparents had. Most people reading *The Secret to Selling Yourself Anytime, Anywhere: Start Bragging!* will have seven or more jobs in their lifetime. It's important to always be prepared!

Take time for yourself, now, to clarify your life and career goals. When changes happen, how will they impact your career choices? Remember, there may be temporary changes, or they may be long-term. Don't wait until you are unemployed to discover what you really want out of your career.

Here are some things you can do each day to help you in your job campaign.

Walk it out. Walk or run at least a mile per day or do any other type of aerobic exercise that you enjoy. Another fun way to ensure that your body is moving? Use a pedometer. Set a target and achieve it each day.

Talk it out. Talk with a few select and trusted friends or family members. Hire a coach. Talk to the clergy of your religion. Or, commit to seeing a licensed and trained professional on a consistent basis until you have resolved any personal issues. Keep in contact with others via social media venues, and face-to-face! Stay involved in social activities. If you have lost your job, know that many have had similar experiences. They will help if they can. However, engaging in "ain't it awful" sessions will only hurt you and stop others from sharing opportunities with you.

Write it out. Keep a diary or journal. It is not for the benefit of others but for voicing your opportunities and challenges in writing. Studies show that writing it down can make a huge difference. Do not send hate letters or nasty emails.

Luck Is Preparation!

Always be prepared for your next job, promotion, or other opportunities. Develop the skills required, even if you need to pay for the courses, workshops, books, or tuition yourself. Some opportunities may only appear once! After a while, they will stop if you are not ready and willing to do the work required to become prepared. Stop blaming your previous employer if you have not acquired the skills you need. Most companies don't wish to hire someone who does not take responsibility for their career choices.

Additional Items for You to Consider:

- ✓ Keep financial debt to a minimum (preferably, have none at all). Too often opportunities come along that people cannot take advantage of because they can't afford it. Keep your credit scores high and keep your credit report clean. Employers do look at these.

- ✓ Take time to learn new skills (software, Internet, music, gardening, public speaking, writing, negotiating, etc.). Be open to ongoing personal and professional development, even if you need to pay for it yourself. It takes more to learn new things than attending a life-changing event or buying into a spoken concept or watching a master performance and trying to adopt it as your own. Take away one or two insights from these experiences and put together a structure for fulfilling the revelations they gave you. Work with your coach or mentor to ensure you use them appropriately.

✓ Don't burn bridges with your references. Even if you're right!

✓ Don't stretch the truth during interviews: Answer the interviewer's questions appropriately and honestly using your brag statements. Stay away from responding with what you think the prospective employer wants to hear. You will often be wrong. Major career derailment can occur when you get the job only to be fired after a couple of weeks. The employer will be hesitant to provide you with a reference since they feel scammed. I have a client who said, "There is nothing worse than hiring a liar!"

✓ Take time to reassess your life goals periodically. Life does change, and so do your goals, personal and professional needs, and aspirations.

✓ Have clarity about your strengths and weaknesses. Use a qualified assessment to help you clarify them. Go to *SeibCo.com* for recommendations. Every strength has a weakness and every weakness has a strength, depending on the situation, environment, and requirements of the job. By knowing yourself well and being open to inevitable changes, you naturally have a confidence about you that works—which is the true sign of a leader.

✓ Don't be a lone ranger. Ask for help. Be willing to accept help graciously.

✓ Hire a coach or find a mentor. Issues that people would like to discuss with a coach include becoming more effective, developing business and professional savvy, developing confidence, having someone to bounce ideas off of, and handling problems that arise.

Who can be a coach? Many people can be if they're 100 percent committed to your success. Many successful business professionals have their own coaches! Don't get hung up on the person being a certified coach if they've had ongoing success over a number of years.

✓ Get involved in and attend trade or professional association meetings.

✓ Life has a way of getting our attention, particularly when we don't want to listen! When you experience similar challenges with bosses, employees, clients, or if you are bored or unwilling to do your job, hire a coach or therapist! Find out why now, before it's too late to help you with your career choices.

✓ Respect all people you meet, and their opinions and feelings. You can achieve this by listening more than talking, maintaining confidentiality, returning all phone calls within 24 to 48 hours, keeping your commitments and following up quickly, dressing for success, arriving at least five minutes early for each meeting, posting appropriate messages on your social media sites, and having a professionally scripted voice mail message.

✓ Remember, companies hire for their own reason, not yours. You cannot sell (the purpose of the interview) unless you understand their needs (the purpose of networking). Do not burn future bridges by telling employers they were wrong to offer the job to someone else.

✓ Always, always, always go to an interview prepared. It doesn't take that much time to Google the company's name and its products and services, and read the information. Write out questions for when they ask you "Do you have any questions?" (See Chapter 12, "Conduct Your Due Diligence") It's always sad to interview qualified

> candidates who blow their opportunities because they are not prepared or falsely believe they understand an employer's culture, even though they never worked for the company, boss, or team members!

The bottom line: Stop waiting for the perfect time! Many times we're sitting on the sidelines waiting for job or career changes to happen to us. If you wait too long to engage in finding the right job or work for you, the opportunities will diminish. Learn how to brag! Showcase your confidence and credentials by effectively using the interview skills outlined in *The Secret to Selling Yourself Anytime, Anywhere: Start Bragging!* to keep you prepared for your next opportunity.

About the Author

Straight talk with dynamic results!

Jeannette Seibly is an international award-winning executive coach and keynote speaker. For more than 27 years, she has been an expert in guiding 1,000s of *leaders to excel, whether or not they have a leadership title.*

Contact Jeannette at *JLSeibly@SeibCo.com*. Don't forget to listen to her podcasts on Anchor.FM or YouTube.com.

How to Work with the Author

SeibCo, LLC

Straight Talk with Dynamic Results

Executive Coaching program
Working with Jeannette achieves intended results through 1:1 and small group coaching.

Facilitating Teams and Conflict Resolution
Jeannette achieves intended outcomes by working with and through teams.

Keynote Speaker
Jeannette engages the audience, invites participation, and achieves results through her keynotes speeches and workshops.

To learn more about how to work with Jeannette Seibly, visit her website at *SeibCo.com* and sign up for her weekly newsletters.

KTAs

Knowledge | **Talent** | **Achievement**

KTAs

Knowledge	Talent	Achievement

KTAs

Knowledge	Talent	Achievement

CPSIA information can be obtained
at www.ICGtesting.com
Printed in the USA
LVHW081508020622
720304LV00009B/687

9 780984 741557